STAINED GLASS SPIRIT

Becoming a Spiritual Community Where Oneness Does Not Require Sameness

TRACY BROWN

ISBN: 978-1-889819-50-1

STAINED GLASS SPIRIT
Where Many Are One

Stained Glass Spirit

Thriving 21st century spiritual communities are easily compared to strong and beautiful stained glass windows. They are composed of many individual people who come together to create a deep and meaningful experience where everyone works together but each person can ALSO shine as themselves at their best.

- Tracy Brown is the founder of Stained Glass Spirit. After working on diversity and inclusion strategy in organizations nationwide, she created Stained Glass Spirit to focus attention on "attracting diversity and creating inclusion" in spiritual communities.

- The focus of Stained Glass Spirit is to incorporate the spiritual concepts of love, oneness, wholeness and harmony into any attention a church or spiritual community places on diversity or inclusion. The motivation for action is spiritual not political.

- Webinars and teleseminars are offered throughout the year. In person workshops and event support are also available.

- Ongoing programs include a monthly prayer call for inclusion and a podcast series featuring candid conversations about spiritual communities that value diversity and inclusion.

- Visit www.StainedGlassSpirit.net

This book is one part of a trilogy focused on diversity and inclusion in spiritual communities.

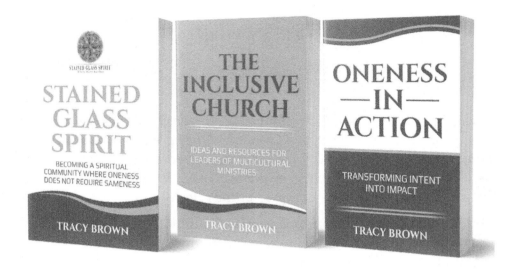

Stained Glass Spirit: Becoming a Spiritual Community where Oneness Does Not Require Sameness (January 2019)
ISBN 978-1-889819-50-1

The Inclusive Church: Ideas and Resources for Leaders of Multicultural Ministries (April 2019)
ISBN 978-1-889819-51-8

Oneness in Action: Transforming Intent into Impact (July 2019)
ISBN 978-1-889819-52-5

STAINED GLASS SPIRIT

Becoming a Spiritual Community Where Oneness Does Not Require Sameness

TRACY BROWN

DEDICATION

This book is dedicated to the individuals who understand the Life of the One can only be fully known through the lives of each one.

This book is dedicated to the people who strive to represent the Love of the One in their interactions with each one they encounter.

This book is dedicated to the faithful who pray for the Harmony of the One to fully demonstrate as harmony linking each one to all humanity.

This book is dedicated to the leaders who recognize the Expression of the One is relying on them to learn how to love the one perceived as the other, then teach others, by their example, to do the same.

This book is dedicated to the spiritual communities around the world that model the Unity and Wholeness of the One by creating the Beloved Community in both form and function by welcoming, valuing, educating, serving and engaging all people.

TABLE OF CONTENTS

INTRODUCTION

What is Stained Glass Spirit?

In a stained glass window, each piece of glass is needed to make it beautiful . . . the same way each person in your Spiritual Community is needed.

Thriving 21st century spiritual communities are easily compared to strong and beautiful stained glass windows. They are composed of many individual people who come together to create a deep and meaningful experience where everyone works together but each person can ALSO shine as themselves at their best.

And when the light of the Sun shines through a stained glass window it illuminates everything in amazing array of color and life. When Spirit shines through each member of your Spiritual community the same thing happens.

Look at each person the way you look at the individual pieces of a stained glass window. Appreciate their differences. Welcome their unique contribution. Nurture their soul and their spirit.

When you consistently allow your best self to be eternally fused with the best of each other person, you will be a part of the Stained Glass Spirit shining within each individual and throughout the entire community.

The Goal

We live in a multi-ethnic, multicultural and multi-generational world. This book explores the concept that leaders in spiritual communities can benefit from paying attention to diversity and inclusion in the 21st century.

This book encourages you to identify the spiritual beliefs you have that mandate you to recognize God in all people.

This book challenges you to distinguish between Spiritual Principle and human socialization in your role as a leader within a spiritual community.

This book is about why you might consider becoming a spiritual community where unity does not imply (or require) uniformity.

The focus of this book is on interaction with, and engagement of, people on the journey to unity and inclusion. This is not meant to ignore the importance of topics related to environmental justice, protection of endangered species, green living or any other movement we might consider in our efforts to create a world that reflects the wholeness of God. However, narrowing the focus on humanity – and how we address the diversity that exists in people who might participate with us on this spiritual journey, is intentionally designed to help you take action and lead more effectively.

Each Section

There are five sections in the book.

1. Diversity is a Divine Idea: God created diversity. God doesn't make mistakes. Diversity is not an accident.

2. Multicultural is (Sometimes) Messy: We don't always know how to navigate all the diversity we encounter in humanity; and that's okay.

3. Inclusion Requires Action: While diversity is normal and unavoidable, inclusion is not. What we do and say will result in either inclusion or exclusion; it is up to us.

4. Walking the Talk: As leaders of spiritual communities, what is required to "put feet to our faith" and demonstrate a consistent message?

5. Intentionally Inclusive: What changes start occurring when we live our commitment to creating the Beloved Community?

Following these five sections, there are dozens of quotations provided. The quotations are grouped by the same five section titles to make it easy for you to find quotations that complement or supplement the content.

Please note that even though the sequence of the sections and chapters are designed to build, it is not required that you read the chapters in the order presented. For a variety of reasons, you may need, or desire, specific ideas related to one section more than another. Or you may have attended a webinar where one section was very clear, but you want to review key concepts in a different section.

Use this book in whatever ways best serve you.

Let's Begin

So, welcome on this journey. Let's explore together what it means to become a spiritual community where Oneness does not require sameness.

DIVERSITY IS A DIVINE IDEA

Biology, Sociology or Spirituality?

The Stories We Tell

Oneness is Not Sameness

"The Universal Mind contains all knowledge and is ever expanding. Spirit experiences Life through each one of us. No two of us is the same."

Ernest Holmes

"Ignoring the beauty and value and uniqueness of different types of people is equivalent to ignoring God and refusing to see all the ways God shows up as humanity. We don't do that with dogs, or flowers ... or trees or clouds or spices or nature or art ... so why would we do it with humans?"

Tracy Brown

BIOLOGY, SOCIOLOGY OR SPIRITUALITY?

Have you ever been in a deep conversation about diversity only to find out, after 20 minutes, that you and the person you were talking with were using the same words but applying completely different meanings to those words?

That happens often when discussing diversity and inclusion. In order to explore this topic, it's important we have a common foundation. So, let's begin with three definitions: diversity, inclusion and Oneness.

Diversity

Diversity is the existence of differences. It includes all the ways we are different from one another. Every person contributes to the diversity of a group or community. Diversity exists and it is neither bad nor good.

Inclusion

Inclusion is the environment or culture we create when we recognize, honor and utilize the diversity within a given group. Inclusion is not automatic; it requires deliberate intention and consistent action.

Oneness

Oneness is the relationship between the Creator of all life and everything it creates. In the context of humanity, each human being is a unique expression of this One Source and cannot be separated from It. Oneness, then, is the natural relationship between God and each human; it does not describe the relationship between two human beings.

The (Merriam Webster) dictionary definition of oneness is "the quality or state or fact of being one: such as singleness, integrity, wholeness, harmony, sameness, identity, unity or union." Because of the nature of this book, we are primarily using the definition of Oneness as a spiritual quality, not the secular definition or interpretation.

You are not required to agree with the definitions above; however, you must understand these three definitions provide the context for how these words are used throughout this book.

Use What Works

When defining diversity, inclusion and Oneness in this way we can easily see there are biological, social and spiritual aspects to consider when working with this topic.

Diversity in human beings is a biological fact. We expect to see, and value, the diversity in the flowers we plant in our gardens, the planets we observe in the galaxy or the animals we view in the zoo. There is no reason for us to ignore (or be fearful of) the diversity in humanity.

Inclusion is not inherent in the existence of diversity. Inclusion (or the lack thereof) reflects the cultural and individual choices we make.

If we are socialized to engage with people who are different from us, we will. If we are socialized to judge, ostracize or fear people who are different from ourselves, we establish or experience separation.

Oneness is a spiritual Truth. It is a Principle that is absolute. When we live our lives from the Truth of Oneness, we are spiritually guided to demonstrate love and respect.

In "10 Ideas that Make a Difference," Ernest Holmes wrote:

> *"The thing that shall establish Unity is that each family group of the race shall respect the individual difference of others, while at the same time cooperating with them."*
>
> Ernest Holmes

In order to create, and sustain, a Stained Glass Spirit spiritual community, there must be an understanding that biology is neutral; inclusion requires human action; and Oneness with God is the kindling that is always ready to feed the fire that burns as the collective Unity between each one of us and our human brothers and sisters.

When discussing diversity and inclusion, we can focus on biology, sociology or spirituality. However, when discussing diversity and inclusion in our spiritual communities, it is imperative we understand, explain and strategize based upon the spiritual mandate for living from the true, essential nature of God.

THE STORIES WE TELL

I was facilitating a large workshop with several dozen people attending. At the end of a small group activity, we were sharing highlights and discussing challenges as a large group. One participant asked, "Why is diversity such a big problem? This is exhausting."

The room got quiet, you know, like so quiet it feels as if every person was holding their breath. It felt inappropriate to reply with a brilliant quote from a social science, psychology or leadership expert. It felt inauthentic to brush the question off as if it were unimportant or disruptive. It felt as if this participant had asked a question almost everyone in the room wanted to ask but either didn't know how or didn't believe it was acceptable.

I took a deep breath, not knowing exactly what words were about to come out of my mouth, and then spoke quietly, but firmly:

Diversity is not the problem.
It is the stories we tell about diversity that are the problem.

I was silent for a few seconds. Some thought I was pausing for dramatic effect. A few came up to me later in the day and shared they were glad I paused because they needed to take in the deep reality that we are our own worst enemies as a result of our stereotypes, judgments and assumptions about people who are different from ourselves.

But the reality is this. In that moment of silence, I was struck so deeply by the fact that the stories we make up are so hateful and damaging that I felt a bottomless and almost debilitating sadness that I couldn't speak.

What I wanted to do was cry. I wanted to retreat to my hotel room and journal and pray and then journal some more. I wanted to run from the room and evaluate whether the work I was doing was even worth it. Who was I to think I could have enough impact to alter a pattern that was so overpowering and prevalent in all of our lives?

Granted, this idea that diversity isn't bad was not new information for me. But I had never articulated it in that way: so succinctly and so clearly. Stripped of paragraphs of academic knowledge and the comfortable jargon of applied behavior science models and systems, the raw truth of our own responsibility for creating and constantly feeding the pain we say we don't want to experience was overwhelming.

The desire, and the commitment, to build Stained Glass Spirit spiritual communities requires us to recognize the stereotypes driving our assumptions, our reactions and our limiting beliefs.

The desire, and the commitment, to build Stained Glass Spirit spiritual communities requires us to recognize we are telling stories that are not the Truth.

The desire, and the commitment, to build Stained Glass Spirit spiritual communities requires us to replace the filters through which we see the world on a regular basis the same way we replace the filters that make the furnace in our home work well or the filters we change in our cars to keep the engine in our car running effectively.

You're correct when you say, "We're all humans." But we are not all the same. The challenge isn't that we are biologically different. The challenge is that we have created - and continue to perpetuate - false and negatives stories about what the differences mean.

The desire, and the commitment, to build Stained Glass Spirit spiritual communities requires us to tell a different story about ourselves, about other people, and about the world we want to live in.

 So, let's change the narrative. Let's tell some different stories about all the ways we are different from one another. Let's flip the script and make diversity a positive instead of a negative.

Will you join me?

ONENESS IS NOT SAMENESS

In New Thought spiritual communities, one of the most challenging conversations related to diversity and inclusion is grounded in a misconception that "oneness" means we are all the same.

More than 10 years ago I was astounded at the answers that came back when I gave an assignment to ministerial students to interview experienced ministers and ask them four very simple questions about the impact of diversity on their leadership decisions, program design, marketing activities and the way they structured the worship experience.

There were a few exceptions, but most ministers included comments like the ones below in their responses explaining why they don't talk about diversity or inclusion:

- "We are both One with God, so we are both the same."

- "We are all One, so I don't need to pay attention to diversity."

- "I don't care about diversity. What I care about is our sameness. We are all expressions of Spirit.

- "Diversity focuses us on our differences, which is uncomfortable; so, we focus instead on things we agree about."

It's 10 years later and comments like this are still alarmingly common.

Ernest Holmes wrote:

"While all people have the same origin, no two
are alike except in ultimate Essence."

Ernest Holmes

When we say that everyone is the same, and we are referring to the concept that we are all created from the same source, that is a factual statement. But there isn't any way to extrapolate that into a viable example that we are all the same in any physical, mental, emotional or cultural way.

Sometimes people argue that God treats all the same or that God "is no respecter of persons" and has an "impersonal" nature. Spiritual Law works the same for every person, which is different than saying every person is the same.

This does not need to be confusing. God treats all the same by applying spiritual attributes to all. God's love has been demonstrated by the creation of each one of us, and all forms of life. God's love is available to all people equally and is demonstrated by that Love providing resources, relationships and opportunities that deliver a life that is uniquely identifiable as that person's life. God treating people equally does not mean treating people the same; it means customizing the absolute principles of God in the specific ways needed for (or used by) each person.

But as human expressions of God, do we demonstrate Love for all people at all times? Uh, no. If we were applying the impersonal nature of God in our relationships with all people there would be a lot less homelessness, hunger, discrimination and trauma in the world.

One way I remember this for myself is to think of my own family.

I am one of three sisters. We have the same parents, grew up with the same last name, the same gender identity and the same race; but I can assure you each one of us is a unique expression of our family's genetics, values, qualities and characteristics mixed with our human experiences based on our personal and professional capabilities.

The ways we are different from one another do not make us any less sisters. We are bonded by our shared heritage without limiting or losing sight of our individual passions, potentialities and paths in the world.

The idea that paying attention to diversity is divisive can often result in us assuming everyone either is just like us or is willing to adjust to our preferred way of thinking, being or behaving. If I am unwilling to explore the needs or desires of people who are participating in the community we are creating, then I will gravitate to doing things the way I like to do them. By designing congregational activities, worship services, community outreach or educational opportunities based primarily on what I think or prefer, I am likely to only attract people who are very similar to me in superficial ways. I am likely to miss building relationships with, and learning from, people who share a deep spiritual commonality but are challenged by things I take for granted as normal, easy or fun.

This also directly applies to those who believe it's more important to focus on things we agree about and avoid topics that generate discomfort.

Leaders in Stained Glass Spirit spiritual communities understand that Oneness is not sameness.

Leaders in Stained Glass Spirit spiritual communities recognize and value the unique characteristics that define individuals.

Leaders in Stained Glass Spirit spiritual communities provide opportunities for different members to demonstrate ways their unique background, culture or experience enhance the community.

Leaders in Stained Glass Spirit spiritual communities develop skills that make talking about diversity a natural part of any conversation related to personal development, leadership strategy or spiritual growth.

MULTICULTURAL IS (SOMETIMES) MESSY

Unintentionally Unwelcome™

Oops! I Didn't Mean to Offend!

Your Learners' Permit

"When any real progress is made, we unlearn and learn anew what we thought we knew before."

Henry David Thoreau

"Our unconscious biases build barriers between us and the people we meet every day. When we are unaware of the ways we demonstrate our biases, we miss opportunities to build bridges with people."

Tracy Brown

UNINTENTIONALLY UNWELCOME™

Even when committed to being inclusive, there are some common – but unnecessary – mistakes church leaders often make.

Often our words and our actions are not quite in alignment. We mean well, but our behavior reveals a conflicting message.

For example, here are four pretty common comments I've heard shared by ministers when they are explaining their commitment to diversity or their approach to inclusion.

- Everybody here loves each other; we don't need to talk about diversity.

- We're very welcoming. We're open to all kinds of people joining our Center.

- We're ready to grow and having more diversity will be a big part of our future success.

- Diversity is important to us; it's one of our values.

But often, the behaviors and decisions send a different message. Let's look at what often happens:

"Everybody here loves each other; so, we don't need to talk about diversity."

The first issue here is that loving each other really doesn't have anything to do with talking about diversity. The minute the minister, or any key leader, in your community makes this statement it sends a message that diversity is considered a taboo topic.

What also happens frequently is the person who makes this statement unintentionally, but habitually, makes inappropriate or potentially offensive comments without realizing their impact. Because they are a member of the dominant culture, they are often unaware of the negative impact of their comments or actions; and they have made it difficult for anyone to correct or coach them because, well, they would have to be willing to talk about diversity in order to understand the issue.

"We're very welcoming. We're open to all kinds of people joining our Center."

One of the common results of this mindset is that people from different identity groups come, they don't return after one or two visits, but they rarely become active participants in your community.

A few generations ago, there was a mindset that everyone should just fit in to whatever the dominant culture was. Simply welcoming people to join your existing culture would be enough. It would be their job to adjust, change or assimilate if they wanted to be accepted and included in any meaningful way.

In the 21st century, that's not very effective. If your ministry is located in an area where there is great diversity, your visitors have many options for their spiritual development and growth.

They have many options where to donate their charitable dollars. And they have many options that allow them to be with people who respect them and provide opportunities to build community together.

And it's important to have clarity about what "welcoming" means. If welcoming people from all identity groups simply means smiling and saying hello when they show up for an event, service or program, that doesn't necessarily translate into demonstrating behavior that makes people genuinely feeling welcome or valued.

Making changes in your welcoming protocol, as well as in your order of service, event planning process, marketing and follow up processes are all needed if you want your behavior to align with your commitment to be inclusive.

"We're ready to grow and having more diversity will be a big part of our future success."

So many church leaders tell me one of the main reasons they want to pay attention to diversity or inclusion is because they are ready to grow or because they really need to grow.

So, I start asking questions about the demographics in the neighborhood around them. I ask questions about the demographics of their current congregation or membership. These questions about demographics are not limited to race and ethnicity. I am curious about demographics based on gender, education, age, economic status and other factors where data is readily available.

I am often surprised that the current population that attends or supports the church is significantly different in multiple ways from the population that lives within a 5-mile or 10-mile diameter from the church location. Living near the church you attend is not a requirement; and, in fact, in many New Thought spiritual communities people are accustomed to driving long distances to participate because there are fewer spiritual communities to choose from.

However, if your spiritual community is not growing, it only makes common sense that the pool of people that match your current demographic is limited. Whether that limitation is a result of distance, theology, age, economic class, or any other factor, the reality is that one of the fastest ways to grow is to serve people who can get to you most easily.

What I see, more often than not, is leaders in spiritual communities spinning their wheels trying to find people just the ones they have always had, who will love the programs they have always offered, and enjoy the music the way it's always been done. I have actually had spiritual leaders tell me it is too much work to change their programming, music, schedule or internal culture to attract and serve people who live down the street, around the corner and are looking for a spiritual home.

When I ask them how they know that or inquire about what attempts they've made in the past (so we can troubleshoot what went wrong) I am usually met with responses that are just their assumptions and stereotypes. It is rare that they have actually engaged with the community nearby to identify what is desired by their closest neighbors and how they might adapt.

One of my favorite examples of this pattern was a ministerial student who shared that after years of attending the church, teaching classes and hosting literally hundreds of events, they had never even had a conversation with anyone who lived across the street or within a block of the church.

But the reason this is one of my favorite examples is because, as a result of taking a class on this topic, they set a personal goal of initiating a few conversations. Those conversations led to that ministerial student recognizing a few very simple things that could be done to be truly welcoming; and it led to a few people who could walk to the church participating in events, programs and classes.

Before those conversations, the neighbors had no idea what a Spiritual Living Center was, and the church had no idea how to respectfully make new friends.

Diversity is important to us; it's one of our values.

Whenever any leader says to me, "Diversity is important to us," I automatically respond with this question: "Why?"

I don't mean to be a skeptic; and I don't like to admit that I have very low expectations; but all too often the response I get is shallow or self-serving.

- Diversity is important to us because it's the right thing to do. (Note: you can't "do" diversity. God has already created diversity everywhere you look.)

- Diversity is important to us because there are so many people who need our help. (Note: your being superior and seeing diversity as a way to help those poor people who couldn't make it without you, is charity work not inclusion work.)

- Diversity is important to us because we want to heal the racism in the world. (Note: Healing racism is an important and valuable mission. Just be sure you understand that race relations, social justice, and social activism are not synonyms for valuing diversity. Race is only one element related to diversity. P.S. any healing that is to be done means you are going to change too.)

- Diversity is important to us because we want to set a good example for the community. (Note: Oh, there we go again, arrogantly assuming we have the answer, and everyone should follow our example. Being a good example does have value; but if your reason for paying attention to diversity is to impress or influence others that might not be the best motivation.)

Less than 10% of the time do I hear responses like:

- Diversity is important to us because our mission is to help all humanity experience their spiritual magnificence, not just people who look, act or think like me.

- Diversity is important to us because God made people of all kinds and we want to worship with all God's people.

- Diversity is important to us because every one of us grows when we meet and build relationships with people who have different experiences than our own.

- Diversity is important to us because we realize when we study, practice and worship with people who are different from us we actually get to see and understand more ways that God expresses in the world.

There's no surprise that when we deflect or avoid diversity in our individual experience, the experience in our spiritual communities reflect that same pattern.

Leaders in Stained Glass Spirit spiritual communities talk about diversity as a way for Oneness to be demonstrated because recognizing diversity is our opportunity to see each person as another Face of God and as a brother, sister or family member to be loved and respected.

Leaders in Stained Glass Spirit spiritual communities challenge themselves, and other leaders, to demonstrate welcoming behaviors based on the cultural needs of the guest, not the cultural preferences of the existing norm.

Leaders in Stained Glass Spirit spiritual communities explore the benefits of diversity and the value of inclusion in the context of both individual and community growth.

Leaders in Stained Glass Spirit spiritual communities ensure that diversity and inclusion are not just words on paper but are also demonstrated in the activities and relationships throughout the ministry.

OOPS! I DIDN'T MEAN TO OFFEND!

Using our own frame of reference, we all occasionally say things that unintentionally send the wrong message.

Most people do not set out to offend others on a regular basis. Most leaders consider the impact of their words and actions on the people they supervise or serve. Most spiritual leaders place a high priority on speaking from a place of love.

So, it's not surprising that we would go out of our way to be intentional in our language when exploring any topic related to diversity or inclusion.

Maybe you've heard – or said – one or more of the following statements to explain why you steer clear of discussing diversity and inclusion:

- I don't want to make a mistake.
- I don't want to make anyone angry.
- I don't want to mess up.
- I want to be politically correct.

If you've said any of the statements above to explain why you don't talk about diversity or try to be more inclusive, then you're focused on the wrong thing!

- Your focus is on making yourself comfortable.

- Your focus is on protecting yourself from embarrassment.

- Your focus is on YOU and not on truly understanding the reason behind the answer you might receive.

The desire to be respectful is important. On the other hand, if you are so afraid you'll use the wrong term when describing someone of a different race, ethnic group, age group, etc. that you don't take any action (or worse, that you feel resentful about the need to be adaptable to different types of people), that really means you don't trust your ability to correct a mistake in a way that is respectful or productive.

What especially concerns me when leaders within spiritual communities find themselves in situations where they have offended others – and there is a cultural element involved - are three things:

1. Ignorance

2. Immobilization

3. Ignoring Responsibility

Ignorance

We live in a time where information is available 24 hours a day literally at our fingertips. Technology allows us to access information about everything with almost no delay.

Every answer to every question can't be found through technology, but technology definitely provides a gateway to basic information that can then be further explored through books, podcasts, workshops, conferences, events, deeper dialogue and expansive conversation with a network of people who are willing to support your growth.

Speaking of people who are willing to support your growth, every leader within a spiritual community should have a carefully cultivated group of people they can talk with about these things. If everyone around you has basically had the same type of experiences with the same kinds of people, how are you going to grow? And who is going to alert you to potential problems in your language, behaviors or leadership decisions? (otherwise known as: "Who's gonna check you, Boo?!")

So, there is no excuse for being ignorant about common phrases, community norms or cultural trends. That's all you need to swim in the shallow waters of daily life.

And, if you are a smart leader, you will be proactive in creating a team of trusted colleagues or advisors you can rely on to help you navigate deeper or choppier water related to specific situations or conflicts.

When leaders in multicultural, multiethnic and multigenerational communities hide behind a fear of offending others, it reflects a choice to be stubbornly ignorant and to stagnate personal growth.

Immobilization

If you are trying to protect yourself from making a mistake to avoid embarrassment, get over it! It is impossible to always know exactly what to say or do in every situation. And no one expects that would.

What is expected is that you are conscious of basic trends and norms and are respectful in your choices for language or behavior. But even then, you are not guaranteed to be right in every situation.

Let's focus on language for a minute. Whatever term you choose in one setting might not be effective in a different setting. For example, I find African American is preferred in most large cities in the United States; but when I am in the southeast black folks tend to prefer the adjective "black."

How did I learn this? By using African American consistently while leading a seminar and having two people come up to me during lunch to say they never described themselves that way because they didn't feel like they came from Africa.

I checked this preference out with a variety of people and confirmed the pattern. And now I'm intentional about alternating between both terms when I don't know for sure if there is a preference with the group I am with.

This reminds me that often there is no single correct answer. Stop being afraid of making a mistake and focus on making honest, authentic connections.

Ignoring Responsibility

In New Thought spiritual circles there is a big focus on personal responsibility for creating a life that works and a life you love.

Yet, I am shocked at how often spiritual leaders fail to take responsibility for comments they make or actions they take that reflect insensitivity toward or ignorance of their impact on people from identity groups different from their own.

I promise I am not about to go on a rant here. I promise I am grounded right now in sharing this only to explain a pattern we all want to avoid.

A very common phrase used in corporate training and community organizing is: "Intent ≠ Impact." It basically reminds us that just because our intent was positive it is less important that the negative impact that occurred.

When we are teaching spiritual principles, we often tell our students that spiritual law is always working, whether we are aware of it or not. Ignorance of the law does not keep it from working.

In the context of diversity and inclusion, ignorance of the offensive nature of a word we use or an action we take, does not make it any less offensive. Whether something is offensive or not is based on the eye (or the experience) of the receiving party or group.

Typically, if someone lets you know you have said or done something that was offensive, it is someone you have either an ongoing relationship with or they are a member of a key stakeholder group. Failing to take ownership for your role in the conflict or misunderstanding is equivalent to telling them they don't matter to you.

For example, this is not the time to be defensive. And it is also not appropriate to tell them:

- it's their problem; or

- they must have attracted it; or

- they must have a chip on their shoulder if that set them off; or

- they need to go do their spiritual work, so they won't be offended in the future when people say or do things with good intent.

While all four of these things might be revealed as triggers holding a client back from their desired goals in the context of a spiritual coaching or counseling environment, when someone is giving you feedback about your behavior, you don't get to let yourself off the hook as if you are a superior spiritual being who never does anything that has negative impact on others.

In the realm of human interaction, we most effectively use our spiritual tools to support us as we navigate through the challenge or conflict we find ourselves in. We don't use our spiritual tools to ignore our responsibility to learn, lead or love.

YOUR LEARNERS' PERMIT

I often share this story about my favorite uncle. One day I opened my email inbox and there it was: an email from my Uncle Paul. Well, at least that's what it looked like. His middle name was very unusual and the email sender column listed his entire name.

But I was confused. My uncle was 89 years old, retired for more than 20 years and had never used a computer. And because he wasn't a computer user, I was pretty sure I'd never given him my email address. My brain said: "This must be SPAM."

I started to delete the email, but then I thought, "Who would know his full name? This must be a joke from a cousin or other relative." So instead of just deleting it, my curiosity won. I opened it.

The first word of the email was "Surprise!" followed by a very short message that made it clear this email was, in fact, from my beloved Uncle Paul.

That happened more than 20 years ago but I remember it so clearly it could have happened yesterday. The concept "You are never too old to learn new things" became clearly embedded in my heart and soul that day.

When you started to drive did you first have to qualify for a Learners' Permit? Most of us took the written test, grabbed the learners' permit and jumped behind the wheel thinking we knew everything we needed to know about driving. We had been watching other people drive for more than a dozen years. We studied the book about driving. How hard could it be?

But it didn't take long for us to realize thinking about something, watching others do something or wanting to do something is completely different from LEARNING to do it ourselves.

When I am leading workshops related to diversity and inclusion, I often find myself giving participants a "Learners' Permit" so they will feel more comfortable stretching beyond their comfort zone to learn new information and try new things.

When you have a learners' permit you understand you have a basic level of competence that allows you to be on the road. At the same time, you understand there is still much for you to learn and practice.

It's the practice part that builds both our confidence and our competence. You don't become an excellent driver without hours and hours of practice. You don't become an excellent driver without hours and hours of coaching from people with more experience. You don't become an excellent driver without making a few mistakes and learning what to avoid, or what to pay attention to, the next time you are in a similar situation.

Likewise, you don't become a confident and competent leader of a Stained Glass Spirit spiritual community without practice.

Rev. Brian Akers talks about this kind of practice as holding himself to a standard of "unrelenting vigilance" related to his assumptions and how his assumptions are reflected in his language, his choices and the impact he has on others.

As leaders in spiritual communities we must have unrelenting vigilance for our own behavior. Too often, people who are passionate about valuing diversity and creating inclusive organizations make the mistake of becoming diversity "cops" instead of diversity "coaches." They learn a little; they clean up some of their previously unintentional mistakes; and then they start becoming vigilantes to correct everyone else.

> *Let everyone sweep in front of his own door, and*
> *the whole world will be clean."*
>
> Johann Wolfgang von Goethe

Accepting a learners' permit reminds us to each pay attention to our own behavior. Our behavior then becomes an example for others. Our growth becomes an inspiration to others. Our commitment to holding ourselves to a high standard – and sharing both our success and our failures – demonstrates high integrity and builds trust.

When my Uncle Paul was 89 years old, he said, "Everybody's always talking about this internet thing. I don't know what it is, but I want to know how to get in on it." He signed up for a series of classes at his local senior citizens' center, asked a ton of questions and practiced almost every day.

Uncle Paul gave himself a Learners' Permit and expanded his horizons beyond anything he had ever imagined. How will you use your Learners' Permit to explore the intersection of diversity, spirituality and inclusion?

What do you need to learn to be an effective leader of a Stained Glass Spirit spiritual community?

What would you like to do differently to demonstrate your commitment to valuing diversity?

How will you apply the concept of unrelenting vigilance to improve your reputation as an inclusive leader and to inspire others to do the same?

INCLUSION REQUIRES ACTION

Diversity Welcome Factor™

Inclusion Worship Factor™

Hard Truths for Team Leaders

"Well done is better than well said."
Benjamin Franklin

*To be an upstander you must wake up, suit up,
show up, and speak up. Be an example of what it
means to raise the vibration and lift up humanity.*

Tracy Brown

DIVERSITY WELCOME FACTOR™

Since 2009, I've challenged leaders in spiritual communities to evaluate their "Diversity Welcome Factor™" in order to identify specific opportunities to be more welcoming. Whether you are welcoming people to services, events or classes, you can pay attention to three things:

1. What is the motivation for welcoming people who are visiting our spiritual community?

2. How do we manage the welcoming process to ensure the needs of multicultural, multi-generational and multi-ethnic guests and members are met?

3. What specific process do we use to meet and greet people that reflects our culture and honors the cultural needs of others?

Motivation

A successful Stained Glass Spirit spiritual community links all welcome processes to the bigger goal of being inclusive.

A successful Stained Glass Spirit spiritual community models inclusion as a representation of Oneness, Harmony and Love.

Management

A successful Stained Glass Spirit spiritual community ensures all staff and volunteers serving as ushers, greeters, hosts, etc.

have a clear understanding that the way they welcome guests and members is a direct reflection of the ministry's commitment to inclusion.

A successful Stained Glass Spirit spiritual community provides training and regular updates to staff and volunteers serving as ushers, greeters and hosts.

A successful Stained Glass Spirit spiritual community audits the performance of ushers, greeters, hosts, etc. to be sure established standards are met.

A successful Stained Glass Spirit spiritual community updates it's procedures and tries different approaches to ensure the commitment to inclusion is met or exceeded.

Meet & Greet

A successful Stained Glass Spirit spiritual community recognizes that all cultures are not based on highlighting individual experience.

A successful Stained Glass Spirit spiritual community has more than one way to identify and acknowledge visitors and guests to accommodate cultural norms and physical abilities.

A successful Stained Glass Spirit spiritual community values the presence of all and finds ways to make that evident with both visitors and regular members.

Five Ways to Prepare Your Spiritual Community for Inclusion

Since paying attention to motivation, management and the way we meet people is larger than the limited activities of a few staff members or volunteers, it is also important to prepare all members of the community to represent your commitment to valuing diversity and ensuring inclusion.

That means that over a period of time, leaders in spiritual communities must educate, inspire and create accountability for the entire membership.

Here are five ways you can subtly – but effectively – help the entire community to accept diversity as a part of the Divine Design and contribute to a spiritual community that welcomes all:

1. Never talk about your mission, vision or values without also talking about diversity and inclusion.

2. In formal messages (from the platform, in classes and at events) explicitly talk about diversity and inclusion. Regularly include examples, stories, quotations and graphics that reflect a healthy respect for diversity.

3. Vary the musical genre, style and performers to reflect the diversity you seek to attract, serve or represent.

4. For classes and events, intentionally vary the formats, delivery styles, use of technology and types of people quoted or held up as examples.

5. Make diversity and inclusion a regular topic for open discussion. And use a variety of methods to collect input and feedback about what they need and how they can support or expand the focus on diversity and inclusion.

Your Diversity Welcome Factor™ is not a static number or a destination that ends a journey. Leaders in Stained Glass Spirit spiritual communities are regularly assessing their current successes, as well as their opportunities to improve.

INCLUSION WORSHIP FACTOR™

Is your message inclusive? Is your music inclusive? Is the way you engage your congregation or participants inclusive (creating a strong sense of membership)?

One of the things I enjoy most is working with ministers, music directors and staff when they are reviewing or revising their standard Order of Service or working on the programmatic elements for worship services and special events.

I developed the Inclusion Worship Factor™ to help identify three specific focus areas that have a major impact on whether your worship service or event aligns with your desire and commitment to be inclusive.

Message

Let's begin with the message. Whether you refer to this as a sermon, a Sunday talk, a homily or an inspirational message, the point is to teach and to inspire. That means you have to reach the minds and hearts or the largest percentage of people possible.

The biggest mistake speakers make with their message is in the examples they share. Since some of the most powerful examples are personal, it is easy to see why we share stories about what we've done or learned in our own lives, assuming our audience will relate to us and learn from our example. This is, in general, a great practice.

However, it becomes a mistake when the examples don't connect to people you are trying to reach. Common mistakes include:

- Overusing examples from professional sports when a large percentage of the listening population doesn't follow those same teams.

- Regularly building stories based on stereotypes, such as women love to shop, and men don't help with housework.

- Using names, locations or socio-economic examples that don't resonate, or even worse, alienate guests or members.

- Coming across as arrogant or superior by only sharing examples that demonstrate personal success.

- Using jokes or humor that puts down a part of the population or a demographic that might not be "in the room" but has people in the room who are connected in a significant way to the group the humor is about.

Many ministers and speakers believe they are keeping their audience in mind as they craft their talks, but when they take the time to ask specific questions they learn that they are missing the mark with more people than they thought.

This is especially important to keep in mind if you are creating a spiritual community that is expanding to include people who have not been a part of the community in the past.

Music

Music is an integral part of almost every service and most events. Music helps to set the mood. Music is a supplemental way to deliver the key message. Music is a key part of engaging the emotional energy of participants individually and collectively. Music is important for managing the flow of a service or event; helping to make the transitions between different parts of the agenda.

So, it's no surprise that music must also be scrutinized for how it supports your commitment to be inclusive.

If the person coordinating the music has very limited exposure to music representing different genres, age groups, cultures and styles, it can counter your desire to be inclusive.

This does not mean your music director must know every possible style and be able to perform it. What is important is that your music director be constantly learning about and connecting with congregants, musicians and community members to identify and meet various needs and preferences.

I've worked with music directors who consistently selected music that reflect their personal tastes and watched the level of disengagement (from both music team members and congregation) consistently grow.

I've also worked with music directors who were always surprising the congregation with music from so many different genres that everyone was always excited and curious ... and proud ... to brag about the music at their church to their friends and family members. These music directors used guest artists when necessary; but they also stretched their own performing skills by learning to adapt to different rhythms and styles.

All of this happens, of course, in the context of what is the desired spiritual teaching or core message that is being presented. But over the course of a few weeks or months, you want everyone who attends your service to be exposed to different kinds of music – including music they feel especially connected to or inspired by.

Membership

What makes people feel as if they are members (or could become members) of your spiritual community?

I recently visited a church where I spent most of the service trying to figure out what was being talked about, what was happening at different parts of the service, how I was expected to engage and what was acceptable or not.

When we visit a church, or attend an event hosted by a ministry that is not our normal experience, we don't expect to know everything. But when planning services or events we can take a few extra minutes to consider the visitor who might be looking for a new spiritual home.

For example, how much of your language is jargon related to your theology or jargon related to your local community? Using acronyms and inside jokes and first names of people who are well known in the community does create a sense of membership. But are you conscious enough of how often you do this so you don't end up frustrating people who might want to become insiders?

Is there clarity about what to expect? Is there an order of service? Or are there announcements about what each segment of the service is about; or what's coming up next?

How do people know whether it's okay to stand and clap; or to dance to the music?

If you have a very active congregation where there is a lot of standing, sitting and moving around, have you considered the impact on people with limited mobility? How are they made to feel comfortable and accepted?

These, and questions like them, are part of a standard assessment you should periodically complete with leaders involved in Sunday service, events, and regularly scheduled classes.

Leaders of Stained Glass Spirit spiritual communities change the names, locations, activities and ages of the characters in the stories they tell to reflect a variety of cultural groups.

Leaders of Stained Glass Spirit spiritual communities ensure the music and the musicians reflect as much diversity as possible.

Leaders of Stained Glass Spirit spiritual communities review and assess their Order of Service on a regular basis to look for ways to develop and retain multicultural engagement.

HARD TRUTHS FOR TEAM LEADERS

Ministers are not the only leaders in your spiritual community. Most churches and ministries could never accomplish everything that needs to be done without a strong team of volunteers.

For you to develop and grow a Stained Glass Spirit spiritual community it is critical that your staff and volunteer leaders not only understand the importance of inclusion, but also how you expect them to contribute.

Three Things You Should Tell All Team Leaders

1. We expect you to have diversity on your team.

2. Diversity brings both conflict and innovation.

3. It's not just what you do but also how you do it.

We expect you to have diversity on your team.

Maybe now is a good time to remind you that when we are talking about diversity we are not referring only to race and ethnicity.

Be sure your team leaders, whether staff or volunteers, are aware of the expectation that diversity will exist on every team. In addition to the benefit of generating a broader pool of ideas and tapping into a greater percentage of your congregation, this offers additional advantages. Teams that represent diversity educate people on the broader definition of diversity, and also allows people to develop stronger skills in communication and conflict resolution as they transform diversity into harmony and inclusion.

Diversity brings both conflict and innovation.

You'll notice I said skills are developed along the journey from diversity to inclusion. Most of us have been raised to avoid conflict, not navigate it or transform it into harmony.

If we are lucky, we find ourselves in a long-term relationship with a friend, work team, or romantic partner that is important enough to us to seek out communication techniques and supportive behaviors that require us to both acknowledge our differences and stay committed to each other's success.

But all too often, we don't have these skills. Your team leaders might not have these skills. And even if you and your team leaders have these skills there will be volunteers who don't.

Many years ago, I served on a Board of Directors where the most important behavior seemed to be focused on going along with anything and everything the Board President said or thought. After each meeting I'd find myself in conversations with three or more of the other Board members who questioned or disagreed with our President. But they would not even consider expressing their question or alternative view to the President or to other Board members.

Confused or irritated by my fellow board members who would complain or share a creative idea with me, I often asked, "Why are you telling me, instead of our President or Executive Director?" and their responses usually were similar to, "Because you're not afraid to speak up."

As you might expect, that put me constantly at odds with the President. Within a very short period of time, that resulted in her making it her mission to discredit every contribution I made. She labeled me as someone who was not a team player and blocked as many of the programs and activities I suggested as possible.

I heard many Board members describe this to me or others as a personality clash between the two of us. But the reality is this. This was not about clashing personalities; at least not for me. I had deep respect for the Board President – both the person and the position. However, there were some cultural dynamics affecting this situation.

In general, black people in America are not afraid to express differing or opposing views. Conflict and confrontation are a part of our daily lives, exploration of multiple options is a part of our cultural heritage, and expression of both feelings and facts is pretty normal. Many African Americans are raised to value the contribution of many voices and we are often raised to make a difference in whatever we commit to, based upon the mission or goal that has been established.

On the other hand, the "white" cultural norm generally places a very high value on individual contribution, on hierarchy and on the appearance of being "nice." Being liked by whomever is in power is deemed a strong contributing factor in success. And all those factors add up to a high value placed on going along to get along.

Now, African Americans know very well how to "go along to get along." We've had to do that to survive. But most of us are also raised to deeply value community. We know the value of soliciting and using many different perspectives and have a cultural tendency to include many voices rather than defer to only one voice or perception.

And the expectation of being liked, when generation after generation of your ancestors have been disliked based solely on the color of their skin but not their character or capabilities, leaves many African Americans having a very low need for being liked by the white people they live, work or worship with.

In a Stained Glass Spirit spiritual community, team leaders are prepared to notice and work through conflicts that might seem to be personality-based but actually have a strong influence based on cultural norms and expectations.

Reminding team leaders that diversity brings both conflict and innovation is critical. Team leaders must understand the benefit that can be achieved with diversity. And they must also understand they will be expected to lead the team through the conflict that comes with diversity as well. Team leaders must be given the support they need to access both.

It's not just what you do but also how you do it.

If you have been a leader in a spiritual community, you know it's not always easy to find someone to fill certain volunteer positions. And there are always some volunteer positions that have lots of turnover, so it feels as if you are always recruiting to keep things going.

Sometimes you find yourself relying on a team leader no one can get along with. The complaints are high, but this volunteer gets things done.

Sometimes it's the team leader who has really poor relationship skills and they just seem to upset, insult or offend others on a regular basis.

Sometimes it's the team leader who procrastinates and procrastinates and then, at the last minute comes through with excellent work, but without regard to the impact on everyone else who had to change their schedules, priorities and planned tasks to accommodate this last minute flurry of activity.

In a Stained Glass Spirit spiritual community, these team leaders must be told it's not just what they do, but also how it gets done. If these team leaders are not held accountable, you will lose the trust and engagement of many people who will avoid volunteering at best, and who will leave your community at worst.

Team leaders must lead in alignment with your commitment to be a Stained Glass Spirit spiritual community or they become your weakest link (and the equivalent to a neon-lit exit door) in your strategy to engage all kinds of people.

Four Ways to Uncover Innocent Mistakes

There are many ways to uncover innocent mistakes staff and volunteer team leaders might be making that unintentionally delay or block your desire to be reach and serve a multi-ethnic, multicultural and multigenerational congregation.

Team Stagnation

When you notice a team has the same people on the team year after year, it's time to look a little deeper. Is the team leader only inviting people they know or resonate with? Are the procedures and processes also stagnated?

Team Turnover

Is the team turnover consistently high? Do people join the team but quickly leave? Is the team leader difficult to work with because they don't welcome new ideas or new ways of doing things? Are the procedures and processes overly complex, so that no one wants to join the team?

Graphics Review

Periodically gather all the flyers, postcards, bulletins, posters and other print materials used in the previous six months. If these items tell the story of your church or ministry, who would look at the images, colors and style and say, "This is someplace I would fit in!"

Conversely who might be seeing your materials and get the message that they aren't welcome?

It's easy to apply this when thinking about race, ethnicity and, to some degree, age. But don't forget to think about the subtle message that accompanies small font size and readability. I once received a series of postcards from a local church that was marketing itself in my neighborhood. There was so much text on each card the text was too small to read without reading glasses. A catchy headline and a few keywords would have made me go to their website for more information. Instead I just tossed the cards in the trash.

If you're wanting to relate to people in an urban environment and your written message is about how relevant you are to today's life challenges, but all your graphics are mountains and oceans, there is a conflicting message.

Review all your print materials periodically to ensure you are sending a visual message that is perfect alignment with your verbal message related to diversity and inclusion.

Surveys

Surveys can be a powerful tool that can help you uncover innocent mistakes. You can occasionally send out a detailed survey. But in general, the three rules with surveys related to diversity and inclusion are (1) keep it short, (2) target carefully and (3) share the results.

Survey your visitors, your members, people who are already on your mailing list, ministry team leaders, ministry team volunteers. Survey everyone – but not at the same time!

Three questions are plenty; definitely use no more than five. Keep it very simple. And be careful that your questions are neutral. No one likes to complete a survey where it appears there is a preferred or expected response.

Target different groups throughout the year so you get specific feedback or input that you can integrate into your ministry. When you survey everyone at the same time the resulting data is usually pretty broad. This makes it difficult to analyze and equally difficult to give direction about changes that need to be made.

And don't be afraid to share your survey results. When people hear the results of surveys it makes them believe you actually care about their input and they are more likely to participate (or encourage others to participate) in future surveys.

Leaders in Stained Glass Spirit spiritual communities recognize all leaders must be involved in achieving the goal.

Leaders in Stained Glass Spirit spiritual communities provide clear messages and set high expectations for leaders related to diversity and inclusion.

Leaders in Stained Glass Spirit spiritual communities find ways to measure and track behavior and results to ensure alignment with the bigger goal.

WALKING THE TALK

Outrageous Outreach™

Are You Listening with Political or Spiritual Ears?

Unity Does Not Require Uniformity

"To work effectively as an agent of change in a pluralistic society, it is necessary to be able to connect with people different from oneself."

Beverly Daniel Tatum

"The focus of Stained Glass Spirit is to help you create a deep and meaningful experience where people who are very different from each other work and worship together by demonstrating the principles of love, oneness, wholeness and harmony within the laboratory of spiritual community."

Tracy Brown

OUTRAGEOUS OUTREACH™

When I am leading workshops on Outrageous Outreach™ there are three topics I generally cover:

1. Marketing

2. Meaning

3. Manners

How you market your spiritual community will greatly affect how you are perceived by potential guests and members. It is important to pay attention to the images, language, colors and formats used to spread your message.

How you choose, plan and conduct your outreach activities gives meaning to your commitment to value diversity and create inclusion. Do your community service and charitable activities add to your credibility? Or do they contradict everything you have said is important?

And it's difficult to talk about outreach without investing some time to learn about, discuss and understand how different cultural norms can affect fundamental elements of relationship building. For convenience, I refer to this as "manners" because most of us intend to be respectful when interacting with all kinds of people. The challenge, however, is that our manners are driven by cultural norms. What I consider respectful may not match what you have grown up being taught as respectful. Therefore, if you don't explore expectations and experiences related to building trust, expressing respect, making decisions, resolving conflict, and many other elements, outreach efforts may not be successful.

In outreach, and in every other aspect of relationship building, it is important to follow "The Platinum Rule" instead of "The Golden Rule."

We're almost all familiar with the golden rule and its coaching to treat others the way we would like to be treated. This is good instruction when we are engaging with people who share the same, or similar, backgrounds or norms. This also works when we are referring to broad concepts more than specific behaviors.

However, the platinum rule guides us to treat others the way they would like to be treated. This is important when we are engaging with people who represent a different background or who value different norms. It is also the preferred approach when you do not know the background or cultural heritage of the person or the people you are interacting with.

For example, it is not unusual for us to say, using the golden rule, that I treat everyone with respect. But in order to do so, I need to apply the platinum rule for the specific ways I behave to be perceived as respectful.

Here is an easy example that applies to many spiritual communities.

Goal: Be friendly. Welcome people warmly.

Golden Rule: Hug everyone when you greet them. Keep a big smile on your face. Greet loudly and with enthusiasm.

Platinum Rule: Ask before hugging. Offer a hug but don't require it. Honor physical space and introvert behaviors without judgment. Mirror energetic flow.

I want to share an example that demonstrates several missed opportunities to reinforce the ministry's commitment to inclusion.

Charity versus Collaboration

One of the places our outreach into the community often sends a conflicting message is in the community service, community involvement, charity or mission work we do.

Charity is a good thing. But all too often, our spiritual communities mislabel their charitable works as collaboration.

For example, a church I was consulting with was telling me about how they collaborated with a church in another part of town by delivering food baskets to the church to distribute the week before Thanksgiving. They were excited about how this demonstrated their commitment to diversity; they felt it was proof they could collaborate cross-culturally; they were sure it would earn them credibility with potential new members from their nearby community.

My questions included:

1. Whose idea was it to provide these food baskets?

2. What specific partnership goal does this project address?

3. Are the food baskets distributed to church members in need, or does the church distribute them to non-church members who live in the neighborhood surrounding that church?

4. How are the recipients identified?

5. Is there any follow-up with or ongoing support given to the recipients of the food baskets?

6. Other than delivering the food baskets, how is the success of this initiative measured?

7. Who determines what food is included in the baskets?

What was obvious to me, based on the responses I was given, was that this church had decided it was a good idea to help a neighborhood they had identified as "poverty-stricken" and thought making sure families had a good Thanksgiving dinner would be a positive effort.

Through online research, one member found a church with a website that listed more than a dozen active ministries. The photos on the website made it appear to be pretty large with a regular church attendance of several hundred each Sunday morning. The church had been located in that community for more than 20 years, so it seemed pretty stable.

The next step they had taken was to call and tell the receiving church that they wanted to provide 50 food baskets. They asked, "Could you distribute these food baskets to people in need?" Of course, the receiving church said yes, and the relationship was born.

For three years the initiating church had delivered 50 baskets to the receiving church.

But they had no idea how the baskets were being distributed. They had asked for no input or feedback about the type of food included in the basket; they simply assumed the food they ate for Thanksgiving was what the recipients would want as well. They had not considered whether the gift certificates they provided to cover the purchase of a turkey could even be used (since the store they purchased the vouchers from didn't have a store within 15 miles of that neighborhood, and the closest store available by public transportation was at least 20 miles away and would require 3 bus transfers if the recipient didn't have access to a car). They had never inquired if the baskets were being delivered to people who had access to ovens and refrigeration. They had never been on-site to participate in the distribution of the baskets and meet the people they were helping. They never had considered whether a year-round food program would be helpful. And they never asked the receiving church, "How does this fit in with your priority programs?" or "Are there other ways we might we support your priority projects or programs?"

Charity is important. And valuable. And good.

But it is not collaboration.

Collaboration means all parties have a voice. Collaboration requires sharing, negotiation, disagreement and intentional choices that reflect the agreement of people with different views, opinions or needs.

In a multi-ethnic, multicultural, multi-generational world, collaboration isn't one-sided. It's a beautiful exchange of ideas and intentions.

Leaders of Stained Glass Spirit spiritual communities develop the collaboration skills required to partner with community leaders from different communities and identity groups.

Leaders of Stained Glass Spirit spiritual communities understand the difference between charity and collaboration.

Leaders of Stained Glass Spirit spiritual communities invest their community engagement resources in activities designed to interrupt systemic disparities more than to fix people or put a bandage on symptoms.

Leaders of Stained Glass Spirit spiritual communities spearhead partnerships where all parties have input and all parties benefit.

ARE YOU LISTENING WITH POLITICAL OR SPIRITUAL EARS?

"I come to church on Sunday to get away from the confusion, chaos and politics in the world."

"Why are you talking about political topics from the platform?"

"I left my last church because the minister was always talking about political subjects."

"If you don't stop bringing up all these social justice topics and go back to teaching pure spiritual principle, I'm leaving and taking my tithes with me."

This is a challenge for so many ministers. How do you teach congregants to apply spiritual principles and spiritual practices in their daily lives without talking about what is going on in the world?

If we truly believe that all we are all connected to each other because every one of us shares the same Creator, then we understand it is impossible to live without impacting the life of others.

Unfortunately, all too often ministers and teachers in New Thought spiritual communities have focused so much on how to use spiritual tools to transform the life of the individual, that members of the community have completely missed the message that every one of our individual lives is contributing to the collective consciousness and the collective experience of all of humanity.

And leaders who serve on the board of directors and feel responsible for the financial health of the ministry often concede to pressure from large donors, even when they understand that real-world examples are powerful and important.

Staff and volunteer team leaders don't know how to respond to the questions and complaints of people they know in the congregation, and as a result tension increases and frustration grows.

The responsibility for building the bridge between individual transformation and societal evolution lies firmly in the messages delivered in services and classes throughout the year. If congregants or students only hear about transforming the world in times of exceptional chaos or disaster, it's not surprising that some confusion would occur.

Ministers definitely have a lead role in building this bridge, but they cannot do it alone. Ministers must be sure that they have explicitly prepared as many leaders as possible to understand why these topics are being used and how they are related to the application of spiritual tools in the world.

Board members, members of the ecclesiastical team, staff and team leaders must all be exposed to the spiritual foundation upon which this line of activity is based. Otherwise it can appear that the minister is pushing a personal agenda instead of a spiritual one.

In my opinion, it is serious malfeasance when leadership in a spiritual community fails to teach and model ways to apply spiritual principals and spiritual practices to real-world issues and challenges.

However, in my experience, I have come across very few members of leadership in New Thought spiritual communities who have the awareness, skills, passion and competence to pull this off in a strategic way.

Integration of societal patterns with spiritual practice seems to be a "growing edge" in New Thought ministries in the U.S. and Canada. In other parts of the world it is often still an after-thought instead of an active strategy.

But it is must be noted that the application of spiritual philosophies to societal challenges is not new. There are dozens of examples of New Thought philosophers and leaders engaging in the social issues of their times.

Ralph Waldo Emerson was a regular voice speaking and writing about anti-slavery during the abolition of slavery. He modeled the teaching of being "for" something (dignity and freedom) instead of fighting against a wrong.

Henry David Thoreau refused to pay his poll tax as a personal protest against slavery and the Mexican War.

Ernest Holmes took a stand in the 30s to ensure blatant racism would not go unnoticed or grow unchecked within Religious Science.

Leaders and youth from Unity and Religious Science communities participated in marches, demonstrations and other events during the U.S. Civil Rights Movement in the 1960s as a demonstration of bringing the spiritual energy of love, freedom and harmony to life.

Applying our spiritual practices to both individual and societal transformation is a documented part of our heritage.

Let me be clear. I am not talking about telling a congregation how to vote or what political party to support. I am not implying that an individual leader's political preferences should be dictated to the membership.

I am referring to using the strife and pain and fear and confusion and discrimination and grief that is so prevalent in today's world as object lessons for shifting both individual and collective consciousness in a powerful way.

I am suggesting that telling the story of a black man killed by police offers and speaking about a national pattern that does not reflect the spiritual truth of love or harmony is important and necessary. Only then can you show congregants how to apply the same principals they use to eliminate undesired patterns in their personal life, to contribute to a pattern changing in their community, workplace or nation.

I am saying that it is equally important to highlight a local, national or international pattern that results in disparate treatment based on gender, or dangerous trends related to sustainability, health and wellness as it is to highlight how an individual can move from dysfunctional, deflated and desperate to become happy, joyous and free.

If we teach that habits can be changed and intentions, supported by consistent spiritual practice, can transform the human experience, why wouldn't we use that same philosophy to benefit the collective experience?

Sometimes I ask, "If we can't talk about, and take action on, these very difficult and often contentious topics with members of our spiritual community, how can we ever expect to talk about them with others in a way that forwards the planet?"

It can be difficult to distinguish between politically-motivated protest and spiritually-mandated strategy. But when we are clear that it is our responsibility to set a new cause into motion that serves as the seed for the spiritual Truth of a world that works for everyone to reveal itself, then, and only then, are we able to take action that is grounded in a love and faith so strong it cannot be denied.

An example of this is the number of spiritual communities that participated in recent Women's Marches in different cities around the world. There were groups from many New Thought spiritual communities who were not there to protest all that has been wrong in the past, but to plant positive intentions and expectations for a future where equity is the norm.

I love that Centers for Spiritual Living has a mission to provide "tools for personal and global transformation" and a vision of "a world that works for everyone." This makes it is impossible to choose only individual good and ignore collective good. We are called to be conscious about the way we live and the choices we make; these things impact both our individual and collective experience.

We are called to be revealers of the spiritual truth and that requires participating in worldly activities. If we want the revelation of good to happen beyond the imaginary and invisible world of our thinking, we must engage in a variety of ways.

One of the best responses to the question, "Why are you talking about political issues from the platform?" came from Dr. Petra Weldes. One Sunday morning, in response to a question asked by a congregant, she explained that it was her job to challenge everyone to apply the spiritual principles we teach in every aspect of their life. She said she always does her best to use real-life examples, whether it's something she experienced with her son or something she is noticing in the national news. She acknowledged that no matter what example she uses each person will hear it based on their own beliefs. And then, in a soft and caring voice, she turned to the entire congregation and asked, "So tell me. Are you listening to me with political or spiritual ears?"

I want to emphasize that she didn't ask this question in a shaming or critical way. There was no arrogance or defensiveness in her delivery. It was a very powerful moment when everyone had the opportunity to check in with themselves and consider their own grounding.

Leaders of Stained Glass Spirit spiritual communities bring spiritual teaching to life by using real-life challenges that people from different cultural groups can relate to.

Leaders of Stained Glass Spirit spiritual communities educate all leaders connected to their church or ministry on the distinction between political activity and spiritual activity.

Leaders of Stained Glass Spirit spiritual communities learn and teach about the legacy of engaging with real-world challenges and societal movements established by our philosophical founders and ancestors.

Leaders of Stained Glass Spirit spiritual communities walk their spiritual talk year-round, not only when there is a crisis or disaster in the world.

UNITY DOES NOT REQUIRE UNIFORMITY

What image comes to mind when you hear or think of the word "unity?"

I've asked that question in many workshops or classes. I've asked people to verbally describe the image that comes to mind. I've asked participants to draw the image. I've asked people to share with a partner, in small groups and even occasionally, in a very large group, to come up to the stage and describe the image they associate with the word unity.

Not surprisingly, the most common image is a circle. Sometimes it is simply the geometric circle, a symbol of continuous flow with no breaks. Often it is a circle of people holding hands. Occasionally the image is one that depicts two or more people hugging.

My follow-up question is often: "Where do you see this kind of unity demonstrated in your world?" Common responses:

- In my family. We are very close.
- At sporting events when we are all cheering for the same team.
- At church during worship services or when we are doing community service.
- My team at work; we work together flawlessly.

It is very rare that someone will describe a group of people with everyone being the same. With family and the blood connection, there is a tendency to think everyone is "the same" but deeper thought reflects the differences within the same family of origin based on genetics, gender, generations, sexual orientation, physical abilities, personal interests and more.

By the time I get to the question, "Does everyone have to be the same in order to have unity?" it requires no thought from participants. The immediate answer is always, "No!" or "Are you kidding?" or "Of course not!"

> *"It is necessary for us to see that unity does not mean uniformity and that the changeless nature of the original Mind in no way imposes monotonous action upon it."*
>
> Ernest Holmes

When we look at the world in general, it is easy to think that someone who looks very different or has a very different background will be difficult to communicate with, work with or worship with.

This does not have to be true.

It is important to ask ourselves why we assume someone must be like us to understand us, to interact with us or to have our best interests at heart.

It is important that we recognize when we are projecting false barriers and building unnecessary walls to separate ourselves from others.

It is important for us to be willing to see how often we are, in fact, pushing others away to protect ourselves from exploring, understanding, experiencing and learning from people who have much to offer.

As leaders in spiritual communities, we often create an image in our minds about "our kind" of people. Anyone who has ever taken a marketing class is well versed in the importance of identifying your target client (or, in this case, your target congregant or community member). This can be very helpful for marketing, and equally harmful if the target market is solely defined based on physical or cultural characteristics.

It is almost a given that a spiritual community would include in its target market people who are interested in, or committed to, applying spiritual principles in their life.

So how do you find people who fit that general classification?

What I hear is: yoga studios, meditation centers, nature lovers who hike, run or are going to sustainable living meet-ups.

I have absolutely no problem with that list. But if your spiritual community is predominantly white with an average age of 55 or older and you have said you want to grow the multi-ethnic population or the multi-generational population your ministry serves, this list needs a little tweaking.

You might still seek relationships with the same type of person but in different parts of your city or through an active digital presence. You will need to ask yourself, how is spirituality developed or expressed in different communities of color?

What do urban dweller do to engage with and honor nature? How do we build strong relationships and partnerships with those who identify themselves as "spiritual but not religious?"

One pattern that has been very well established in New Thought spiritual communities is related to African American congregants. A very large percentage of black people in New Thought have an extraordinary bond with their cultural heritage. They understand their ethnic history. Many have studied African and afro-centric philosophies and religions. Most are well-grounded in the strengths of their cultural background. They are not joining New Thought communities to replace that, but instead, they often discover New Thought philosophy beautifully aligns with the deep, spiritual grounding of African culture. They are joining New Thought communities to integrate the ancient with the contemporary in order to live powerful and meaningful lives in the current world.

If you are serious about developing a multicultural community that works, you will be required to look where you've never looked, go where you've never gone and be who you've never been.

Isn't that what we teach? If you want to transform your life, as an individual, we show you not only how to think differently, but also how to choose differently and then behave differently to create a life that is in alignment with your intentions.

Being a leader in a Stained Glass Spirit community is no different. The community will only grow toward that intention if beliefs drive behaviors, behaviors become habits and habits generate a transformed outcome.

Leaders in a Stained Glass Spirit spiritual community meet, and get to know, many different types of people.

Leaders in a Stained Glass Spirit spiritual community are able to distinguish between target market and current membership.

Leaders in a Stained Glass Spirit spiritual community challenge board members and team leaders to expand their assumptions about the physical attributes of their church or ministry.

Leaders in a Stained Glass Spirit spiritual community create an inner circle of friends and advisors that represent diversity in order to expand their personal comfort zone with cultural differences.

INTENTIONALLY INCLUSIVE™

Where Many Are One

A World That Works for Everyone

Every Day is a Donation to Eternity

"It is certain you will have to love your fellow man if you wish to be happy. This does not mean you love those who are closest to you any less; you merely love all humanity more."

Ernest Holmes

"A Stained Glass Spirit community is one where each person is recognized as a unique expression of God and their individual strength and beauty become essential elements that contribute to a lively and inspiring collective experience."

Tracy Brown

WHERE MANY ARE ONE

One of the tag lines associated with Stained Glass Spirit is "where many are one."

Some people has asked me if this was a nod to the United States motto of "E Pluribus Unum" which translates from Latin into English to mean: out of many, one. It wasn't.

For me, the U.S. motto implies that out of many, we can behave as one. We can come together as one. We can unify to be one group, one people, one nation.

The Stained Glass Spirit tag line "Where Many Are One" starts from a spiritual foundation that all together the many are the physical representation of The One, God. We are already One. We are already equal. We are already whole.

What would our world be like if we went through our day with the understanding that each person we meet is God expressing and experiencing life? *I am God expressing & experiencing life. No more - No less.*

What would our relationships be like if we interacted with the people we encounter recognizing them as equal because we are both creations from the same source of all life?

How quickly would our daily frustrations dissolve if we remembered we are already connected to each other, and to life itself, because we've been created by the same Love?

There is an ancient African philosophy that has become more known and understood in Western culture during the last 20 years after Bishop Desmond Tutu wrote about it in his book, "No Future Without Forgiveness." This concept of "ubuntu" basically means I exist because of you. The literal translation of the word is "humanity." The common explanation of it's use as a greeting is the philosophy that ubuntu means 'I am, because you are."

Ubuntu is a common greeting in South Africa. But it is more than a greeting; it is a Zulu philosophy; it is a cultural way of being in the world. This idea that each one of us is interdependent on the life and experience of every other person we encounter is foundational to building truly inclusive cultures and spiritual communities.

You may also be familiar with the greeting, Namaste. Namaste is a Sanskrit word which literally translates to "Salutation to You," but is often described to mean, "The Divine in Me Bows to The Divine in You."

Since Namaste is very popular and almost universally recognized as a loving and respectful greeting in spiritual communities, I have developed a closing activity that has received exceptionally positive feedback from participants in a variety of workshops and events.

From Namaste to Ubuntu

In this activity, participants choose partners and go through a 4-step process with each other.

> Step One: Look your partner in the eyes. Say Namaste. Bow. Make eye contact and smile.

Step Two: Hold hands while making eye contact and take a deep breath together.

Step Three: Hug and whisper, "Ubuntu."

Step Four: Step back. Make eye contact. Then move to a new partner.

This "From Namaste to Ubuntu" closing practice is especially powerful at the end of a dialogue or workshop where the conversation has been focused on creating inclusive environments. It viscerally bridges the gap between independence to connection to interdependence. It helps participants move from thinking about inclusion and oneness, into experiencing what it feels like to truly see, accept and love another person as an essential part of one's own life.

The idea of "Where Many are One" is also strongly reflected in indigenous cultures where family, community and group identity is the norm. It is not that individuals seek to come together, but the assumption is that the starting place is unity, harmony and kinship.

Stained Glass Spirit spiritual communities are the place where diversity, spirituality and inclusion intersect.

Stained Glass Spirit spiritual communities warmly greet the stranger with a deep knowing that there are no strangers, just brothers, sisters and family remember returning home.

Stained Glass Spirit spiritual communities see the beauty in the person who looks different, speaks different, and demonstrates different life experiences.

Stained Glass Spirit spiritual communities accept that God is calling them to see – and serve – the entire expression of humanity, not just the ways that are comfortable or duplicative of their past experiences.

Stained Glass Spirit spiritual communities are havens for The Beloved Community so beautifully described in the writings of Dr. Howard Thurman and Dr. Martin Luther King Jr.

you are safe
here

A WORLD THAT WORKS FOR EVERYONE

Have you heard your spiritually grounded friends or relatives or church members say things like:

- "I don't like politics. It's mean, unfair and not in alignment with my spiritual principles."

- "You can't trust any of the politicians or even the media. It's a mess!"

- "I'll just ignore politics and focus on love."

- "Let's not talk about racism. It's sad and embarrassing and besides, we're all just one race: human."

- "All that talk about race and Black Lives Matter just divides us. Besides, it doesn't have anything to do with me; I'm not a racist. I'll just hold a vision for peace."

Wait. Stop. Hold on.

These are examples of spiritual bypass at work. Using spiritual principles to escape the world is not what we are called to do. Our spiritual principles and practices are designed to keep us connected to our divinity while we navigate our human experiences.

What is Happening Anywhere is Happening Everywhere

When did we forget that what is happening anywhere is what is happening everywhere and it's actually impossible to separate ourselves from the pain, confusion, anger, fear, disparities, hatred and violence that is so prevalent in our world today? There is NO spot where God is not. God is just as ready to be revealed in the messy parts of human life as in the serene parts of human life. God is in the entire range of experiences.

You Are Meant to Be an Agent for Positive Change

When did we forget that God does things for us by working through us? If those of us who have deep spiritual awareness refuse to be used as agents of transformation, then the opportunity to awaken humanity is left in the hands and hearts of those with limited belief in the power of love, joy, peace, harmony and wholeness to reveal itself as the true nature of life. Since we know change is always happening, that means whatever transformation occurs will then reflect their deepest beliefs and will expand the fear, anger, revenge, hatred, distrust and violence we already have.

We can put our heads in the sand, like an ostrich, and pretend hatred and disrespect are not happening because we refuse to look at it. We can put our thumbs in our ears, wiggle our fingers, close our eyes and sing, "I can't hear you," but that doesn't mean the very loud noise of hatred, violence, protests and politics isn't happening.

The foundational beliefs of New Thought in general, and Science of Mind specifically, call us to apply spiritual principles in all aspects of life. And, actually many of us do that in most parts of our lives. But for some reason, we get triggered with politics and other highly charged topics and run away from our responsibility to show up as examples of spiritually grounded Light right in the middle of what appears to be darkness.

You are being called to be a part of the healing. I am being called to be a part of the healing. We all are being called to step up and live in ways that represent and expand love.

The demonstration of Oneness occurs when we treat the many the same way The One treats each individual.

Maybe your example is Jesus, the Master Teacher, who walked the earth modeling love, forgiveness and peace. Or perhaps you seek to follow the example set by Martin Luther King Jr, Mahatma Gandhi, Mother Teresa, Buddha or your favorite Uncle Bob. Some of my most powerful examples were people who were not famous, not elected and not paid to be change agents.

Words + Action = Transformation

For most of us, the examples of powerful change agents we look up to did not disengage from the world. Instead, they consistently brought their understanding of spiritual Truth forward into situations rife with conflict, disparity, pain, loss or mistrust. Their words and their actions raised the bar for what behavior, what policies, what practices and what strategies would be required for us to demonstrate a more positive future.

You probably already have experience doing this in some aspects of your life. Can you think of some part of your life where there has been some controversy or disagreement, yet you have found a solution that addresses the issue while still being engaged in ways that align with your values or beliefs?

- For example, I have friends who don't like to shop at Walmart because Walmart's employment practices are not in alignment with their spiritual principles. These friends still need affordable food, clothes, household goods and cleaning supplies as part of their physical/human experience. So, they shop at other stores or expand their garden or buy online.

- Some friends don't like that the Boy Scouts of America denies leadership opportunities to men who identify as gay. This is not in alignment with their spiritual principles. So, they have found other ways for their sons or grandsons to learn life skills in environments that are respectful of diversity based on sexual orientation or gender identity. They also make sure to give these boys a clear message that people are not to be excluded based on sexual orientation.

- Other friends don't like the way the school board runs their city's educational system because the haves and have nots are not treated equally. This is not in alignment with their spiritual principles. Some of them home school. Some are able to afford private schools. But many send their beloved children to public school anyway, because they want them to be exposed to a wider variety of children, cultures, and families. They carefully choose the school, then they get personally involved in the parents' organization or make time to volunteer each week or month to ensure the teachers and administrators at the school are supported and encouraged.

What these, and so many other examples have in common, is the choice to take visible, tangible, positive action that represents what we believe. We don't pretend the controversial issue or broken system doesn't exist. We don't disengage. And we typically don't go on an all-out campaign to fight against what we don't like about the situation.

Instead, we get the information we need, we research the alternatives and we then take whatever action seems to be more in alignment with the positive outcome we want to experience in our lives.

Ignore. Deny. Hide. The Pathway to More of The Same

So why is it we think we can – or should – hide when it comes to racism or presidential politics or any other topic, we are especially uncomfortable with? We, who are spiritually mature, don't hide from life; we face life, we nurture life, we improve life!

Life is always changing, expanding and moving forward. Our opportunity (and some would say our responsibility) is to contribute to Life moving forward toward that which is the best and highest good for ourselves individually and for all humanity.

Ernest Holmes reminded us, in Sermon by the Sea, "How important it is that each one of us in his simple way shall live from God to God, with God, in God and to each other." The spiritual path requires us to do our inner work and to also be fully engaged in presenting the fruits of our inner work in the outer world.

Change is always happening. When we – who are spiritually grounded and guided – fail to engage with the topics and themes that are challenging our communities and our nations, we leave the arc of change to be completely influenced by those who believe in duality, pain, negative use of power and control through fear or violence. When we fail to engage, we are actually withholding the love, peace, joy, balance, harmony and wholeness of Spirit.

No amount of silent prayer, individually holding a vision or denying what is happening in the world will create change if those spiritual practices are not matched with physical action. Clear intention countered by fear, false belief or failure to act results in zero (or limited) change. However, clarity of purpose combined with conviction in action creates the life-changing transformation we desire.

So often we say we believe Ernest Holmes' words: "There is a Power for Good in the Universe and It is available to all." But often our actions are communicating: "I'll just keep all that good stuff for myself and I don't care if others have it. Let them find their own way."

Judgment, Shame and Blame are Counterproductive

When we encounter others, who have a different experience that our own, or when we are forced to look at societal pain, instead of recognizing patterns that can be broken and habits that can be replaced, we find ourselves passing judgment from a place of superiority and blaming others for physical and economic conditions that have little or nothing to do with individual mindset or capability. Nowhere is this more evident than when we criticize groups of people for the conditions they experience that are actually beyond their individual control and reflect cultural norms (or cultural consciousness).

In Science of Mind we do not teach that we individually control all conditions, but that we can influence the trends of the types of conditions in our lives. We also teach that through our thoughts and beliefs we can always control our response to the conditions we find ourselves in.

So, the true trademark of spiritual strength and spiritual maturity is demonstrated in the person who steps into the game of life so solidly grounded in spiritual Principle that they are able to show up over and over again in the most difficult situations without completely losing themselves to the human weaknesses of fear, pettiness, judgment, anger, competition or revenge.

We don't learn to do this by hiding from controversy, pain, anger or fear.

Refuse to Run Away

The next time you, or someone you care about, is tempted to ignore, deny or hide from that part of 21st century life that is challenging, refuse to run away.

Consider this: maybe you are triggered by this situation because you are being tapped to be a part of the healing. Maybe you are the one who will be the revealer of Truth that provides the tipping point for love and peace to take its rightful place in our human experience. Without your contribution, the tipping point might not be reached, and the awakening of humanity will be further delayed.

None of us are required to run for office, lead a major protest, create a new political party or be on the evening news each evening speaking out against hatred, violence, disrespect or abuse of power. These are great options for those who are drawn to serve humanity in that way. But every one of us has many ways we can be consistent examples of hope, love, respect, compassion and harmony. Even when the topic is racism or politics.

Let's commit to be the best in humanity today, and every day.

Now is the time to transform your love from silent, mental attitude into strong, measurable action!

Now is the time to set an example for mutual respect and collective success.

Now is the time to deliver on our promises of peace and harmony for all nations.

Now is the time to get involved in public or political activities to ensure spiritual principle is integrated into decisions, policies and programs that affect all communities.

Now is the time to speak up and speak out when disparity, discrimination, deceit, or disrespect are present.

Now is the time for us to come together to show that it is possible to operate from love, to create a world that works for all kinds of people.

EVERY DAY IS A DONATION TO ETERNITY

Every day is a donation to eternity.
Even an hour is a contribution to the future.

The Husia

Being intentionally inclusive simply means you have clarity about the positive impact you want to have in our multi-ethnic, multicultural and multi-generational world and you live in conviction with that clarity.

When this is true, every day you make choices that value diversity and contribute to an inclusive church, community or world, you are making a donation to the revelation of the Truth of Harmony, Love, and Peace.

Review the list below. What resonates with you? Which of these practical action items is perfect for you to learn more about right now? Which of these action items is something you want to incorporate into your leadership style? Which of these actions items needs to be practiced by key members of your leadership team? Pick one, or a few, and put them into action immediately!

The list is not meant to be either complete or absolute. It is designed to be a catalyst to your own thinking about ways you can be an effective and inspiring leader of a Stained Glass Spirit spiritual community.

Please note: The list is numbered to make it easier to engage in dialogue about the items. The numbers do not reflect any prioritization or preferred sequencing of actions.

1. A leader of a Stained Glass Spirit spiritual community can easily explain the spiritual mandate for valuing diversity and being inclusive.

2. A leader of a Stained Glass Spirit spiritual community ensures the diversity of the membership is honored and reflected in programs, services, materials and events.

3. A leader of a Stained Glass Spirit spiritual community values different perspectives and is proactive in soliciting and including a multicultural perspective.

4. A leader of a Stained Glass Spirit spiritual community proactively considers the diversity of key stakeholders when creating or reviewing programs, policies and services.

5. A leader of a Stained Glass Spirit spiritual community recognizes tools and services offered must be adapted to reflect the needs, expectations and cultures of the membership.

6. A leader of a Stained Glass Spirit spiritual community educates themself and others on the impact of diversity on programs, policies and services.

7. A leader of a Stained Glass Spirit spiritual community demonstrates sensitivity to a multicultural constituency and is a role model for inclusive leadership behavior.

8. A leader of a Stained Glass Spirit spiritual community is comfortable facilitating sensitive conversations to help

congregants or clients resolve cross-cultural conflict or develop cross-cultural relationships.

9. A leader of a Stained Glass Spirit spiritual community consistently holds committees, work groups and project teams accountable for demonstrating a commitment to diversity.

10. A leader of a Stained Glass Spirit spiritual community requires all hiring and selection processes to include candidates who reflect the diversity of both the spiritual community and the public served.

11. A leader of a Stained Glass Spirit spiritual community considers the impact of all decisions on a multicultural membership.

12. A leader of a Stained Glass Spirit spiritual community has a commitment to continued education and continuous learning about cultural diversity and its impact on relationships with both new and existing congregants.

13. A leader of a Stained Glass Spirit spiritual community celebrates the small successes, rewards risk takers and emphasizes the desired outcome (not the current liabilities).

14. A leader of a Stained Glass Spirit spiritual community relies on a personal inner circle or specifically designated advisory committee to provide both valuable guidance and trustworthy feedback about multicultural, multi-ethnic and multi-generational topics.

15. A leader of a Stained Glass Spirit spiritual community knows they are not perfect and forgives themself when they make a mistake.

What would YOU add to this list?

16.

17.

18.

19.

20.

Your ministry, and the world, need you to be a leader of a Stained Glass Spirit spiritual community. Together, let's create heaven on earth!

ADDITIONAL QUOTATIONS

Diversity Is a Divine Idea

"And he made from one man every nation of mankind to live on all the face of the earth, having determined allotted periods and the boundaries of their dwelling place, that they should seek God, in the hope that they might feel their way toward him and find him."
Acts 17: 26-27

"Unity teaches that each person is a unique expression of God created with sacred worth."
Unity Principles

"The manifest universe is the body of God ... all people are incarnations of the One Spirit."
Ernest Holmes

"God is all there is, and we are direct and beautiful expressions of It."
Katherine Q Revoir

"Most people are perfectly happy being different, as long as they know their difference is not perceived as a deficiency."
Fern Lebo

"Diversity is Divine Infinite variety expressing, relating, shaping, inspiring and transforming your world."
Tracy Brown

"The world in which you were born is just one model of reality. Other cultures are not failed attempts at being you; they are unique manifestations of the human spirit."
Wade Davis

"Since all humans have been created in the image of God, God does not make any distinction between people regardless of race or colour."
Bahá'í Principle

"A renewal in which there is no distinction between Greek and Jew, circumcised and uncircumcised, barbarian, Scythian, slave and freeman, but Christ is all, and in all."
Colossians 3:11

"Only people with petty minds indulge in racial hatreds and distinctions. God's perfect idea of man is the basis for every living soul, and we must believe this and act as though it were so. When we dislike people and groups, we are bearing witness to our small and limited viewpoints. The people in whom we fail to find good are born of the same Mind, operate under the same Law, and express the same Life as we do. Our inability to see their divine origin is our self-created stumbling block. "
Ernest Holmes

"Nothing that God ever made is the same thing to more than one person."
Zora Neale Hurston

"Blackness is the same as whiteness as far as God and truth is concerned. God has all kinds of colors in his universe and has not condemned any color."
Clarence L Franklin

"We humans are similar to each other, but like fingerprints and cultures, not quite the same. So, viva la diferencia and let's get to know one another, born of respect."
Piri Thomas

"After this I looked, and behold, a great multitude that no one could number, from every nation, from all tribes and peoples and languages, standing before the throne and before the Lamb, clothed in white robes, with palm branches in their hand."
Revelations 7:9

"God is like a mirror. The mirror never changes but everybody who looks at it sees something different."
Rabbi Harold Kushner

"The Lord did not people the earth with a vibrant orchestra of personalities only to value the piccolos of the world. Every instrument is precious and adds to the complex beauty of the symphony."
Joseph B. Wirthlin

"The idea of the oneness of God is not a philosophy of absorption or annihilism. We do not become absorbed in the universal Self to the loss of individuality. Quite the opposite. We find ourselves, not absorbed, but immersed, in a Universality, each one being a unique, individual and different manifestation of that which itself is one, undivided, indivisible and whole."
Ernest Holmes

Multicultural is (Sometimes) Messy™

"For him to have understood me would have meant
reorganizing his thinking... giving up his intellectual ballast, and
few people are willing to risk such a radical move."
Edward T. Hall

"We are all a part of one Life.
And we each have our own life."
Tracy Brown

"From One come many. All come from the One, and all live in,
and by, the One. From Unity comes multiplicity, but
multiplicity does not contradict Unity. It is like the soil: we
grow many plants from one soil, but the Unity of the soil is
never disturbed. So, the One Mind, working through the
Creative Medium of the Universe, produces many things."
Ernest Holmes

"You have to tell the truth, even if it's not politically popular or
runs against the racist stereotypes people have been taught.
When you don't, the consequences are far-reaching.
You lay the basis for further attacks against all immigrants and
people of color for the sake of tactical considerations which are
really illusions."
Susan Alva

"Mistakes are a fact of life. It is the response to error that
counts."
Nikki Giovanni

"Begin challenging your own assumptions. Your assumptions are your windows on the world. Scrub them off every once in a while, or the light won't come in."
Alan Alda

"When we come into contact with the other person, our thoughts and actions should express our mind of compassion, even if that person says and does things that are not easy to accept. We practice in this way until we see clearly that our love is not contingent upon the other person being lovable."
Thich Nhat Hanh

"In total, six out of ten twentysomethings were involved in a church during their teen years but have failed to translate that into active spirituality during their early adulthood."
The Barna Group

"When any real progress is made, we unlearn and learn anew what we thought we knew before."
Henry David Thoreau

"In seeking to avoid a fight we concede what we're about. ... We must realize, understand and believe that our current conditions do no reflect our ultimate potential. If we limit our choices only to what seems possible or reasonable, we disconnect ourselves from what we truly want."
Gary Delgado

"Developing acceptance requires you to get out of your comfort zone."
Lenora Billings-Harris

"There is neither Jew nor Greek, there is neither slave nor free man, there is neither male nor female; for you are all one in Christ Jesus."
Galatians 3:28

"Do we not all have one father? Has not one God created us? Why do we deal treacherously each against his brother so as to profane the covenant of our fathers?"
Malachi 2:10

"The future of the earth may depend upon the ability of all women to identify and develop new definitions of power and new patterns of relating across difference."
Audre Lorde

"It is inconceivable to me that a Christian can have a Christ-exalting love for diversity in the church and be hostile toward diversity in the nation."
John Piper

"What you do speaks so loudly that I cannot hear what you say."
Ralph Waldo Emerson

"We may encounter many defeats, but we must not be defeated."
Maya Angelou

Inclusion Requires Action

"There is no individual good. Good belongs to everyone. Good fulfills itself only as it multiplies itself; therefore, there is no good that belongs to you and to me alone, no final peace to us only as individuals. The watchword is not exclusion but inclusion, and the more good we release, the more good we experience."
Ernest Holmes

"I can't change society for you.
I can change society with you."
Sieneke Martin

"I don't need you to be like me to show you respect."
Tracy Brown

"Spiritual activism begins with the personal, yet moves outward, acknowledging our radical interconnectedness."
AnaLouise Keating

"Reconciliation is to understand both sides; to go to one side and describe the suffering being endured by the other side, and then go to the other side and describe the suffering being endured by the first side."
Thich Nhat Hanh

"I don't want violence to have the last word."
Cindy Widell

"I am sure there are things in our world to which we should never be adjusted. There are some things concerning which we must always be maladjusted if we are to be people of good will."
Martin Luther King Jr

"The moment we cease to hold each other, the sea engulfs us, and the light goes out."
James Baldwin

"God speaks to us in the Qur'an saying that He will not change our condition until we change what is in our hearts and souls."
Saleemah Abdul-Ghafur

"There is One Spirit incarnated in everyone, an immortal Presence forever expanding everything, causing everything to grow. What a difference it would make in our human relations if we tried to sense the meaning of this Divine incarnation in all people and adjust our viewpoint to the truth that all are bound together in the unity of God. "
Ernest Holmes

"A church faithful to the gospel is summoned by the Lord of the church to challenge such exclusion and to practice an inclusiveness that is as broad as humanity and as deep as God's generosity."
Daniel Hazard

"In order to move forward we need both the courage of our convictions and the commitment to do the work."
Gary Delgado

"Life is not intended to be safe. A safe life has too small a name for a creature of eternity. Life, at its noblest and highest, has a hazard about it."
Ethel Waters

"We need a moral prophetic minority of all colors who muster the courage to question the powers that be, the courage to be impatient with evil and patient with people, and the courage to fight for social justice."
Cornel West

"I'm sorry; wherever there's injustice it's your duty as a human being to speak up and if you don't, there's no excuse. You're just a lemming. So, if you don't speak out against injustice, you're a lemming."
Russell Means

"It ain't nothing to find no starting place in the world. You just start from where you find yourself."
August Wilson

"And when we are able to reach out beyond the indifference and the coldness of life, reach through all intolerance and unkindness, only then do we meet that Divine center which is forever established within every person."
Ernest Holmes

If even lifeless instruments, such as the flute or the harp, do not give distinct notes, how will anyone know what is played?
1 Corinthians 14:7

Walking the Talk

"Wisdom is not a fixed quality. It circulates among us."
Sister Souljah

"When you've got so much religion that you can't mingle with people, that you're afraid of certain people, you've got too much religion."
Clarence L Franklin

"Don't tolerate me as different. Accept me as part of the spectrum of normalcy."
Ann Northrop

"If once we let ourselves get past the outward appearance of the individual, we come to understand that Life at the center of his being is the same as at the center of our being."
Ernest Holmes

"Ain't no such thing as I can hate anybody and hope to see God's face."
Fannie Lou Hamer

"A new commandment I give to you, that you love one another, even as I have loved you, that you also love one another. By this all men will know that you are My disciples, if you have love for one another."
John 13:34-35

"We talk about it from the pulpit: being gay and lesbian and still being able to love God and know that God loves us. Our church's motto is "God loves you just as you are."
Rev. Janyce Jackson

"In our meditation for friendship, let us make our unity with all people, all life."
Ernest Holmes

"Movements for change, movements to make us well, to create healthy societies – whether tribal or American – are grounded in healing, are grounded in honesty."
Winona LaDuke

"There is no doubt, however, that the deepest impulse of the Bible is toward inclusion, that all of God's creatures be accorded dignity, respect, safety and a sense of belonging. That deep biblical impulse gives the church its primal mandate."
Daniel Hazard

"There are no degrees of human freedom or human dignity. Either a man respects another as a person or he does not."
James Cone

"But together—in all of our beautiful, messy, glorious, chaotic diversity—we can be part of a robust movement that not only proclaims the message of God, but also displays the magnificent image of God to people of every nation, tribe, and language. And when we do that, we get a little bit of heaven right here on earth."
Wes Foster

"Progress lies not in enhancing what is, but in advancing toward what will be."
Kahlil Gibran

"All churches say they are welcoming. What that means, though, becomes more apparent in their practices and attitudes."
Stacey Simpson Duke

"It's not that the sense of separateness is not authentic, but merely that it is not absolute."
Howard Thurman

Intentionally Inclusive™

"It is impossible to experience your oneness with Spirit without loving, valuing, respecting and embracing diversity."
Tracy Brown

"If you see God in each other, there is love for each other, then there is peace."
Mother Teresa

"Once the neighbor is defined, then one's moral obligation is clear."
Howard Thurman

"Only one thing registers on the subconscious mind: practice. What you practice is what you manifest."
Grace Spear

"We find ourselves, not absorbed, but immersed, in a Universality, each one being a unique, individual and different manifestation of that which itself is one, undivided, indivisible and whole."
Ernest Holmes

"It is all about love that knows no boundary of geography or country; it is simply a generation's commitment to what service to humanity is all about."
Cecile Caguingin Ochoa

"All men belong to each other, and he who shuts himself away diminishes himself; and he who shuts another away from him destroys himself."
Howard Thurman

"All places and all beings of the earth are sacred. It is dangerous to designate some places sacred when all are sacred. Such compromises imply that there is a hierarchy of value, with some places and some living beings not as important as others. "
Leslie Marmon Silko

"The spiritual components of life cannot be divorced from politics, sexuality, writing, or daily living."
AnaLouise Keating

"It is certain that you will have to love your fellow man if you wish to be happy. Your union with God implies your union with everything that lives ... This does not mean that you love those who are closest to you any less, you merely love all humanity more."
Ernest Holmes

"Grace is the ability to redefine the boundaries of possibility."
Manning Marable

"I am not a special person. I am a regular person who does special things."
Sarah Vaughn

"Only love overcomes the fragmentation of human nature."
Maximus the Confessor

"The world is before you and you need not take it or leave it as it was when you came in."
James Baldwin

"I do not care very much for the word "tolerance" as though we tolerated each other. That is better than intolerance, but people who are tolerant because they have made up their minds to be tolerant are missing a lot. "
Ernest Holmes

"In the religious community, we think in generations and that's the way to think because that's how real change happens."
Alexia Salvatierra

"Circumstances do not create themselves; they are always molded by someone's thought patterns. In the collective life they are molded by the sum-total of all persons' thoughts; in our individual lives they are molded by our own personal reactions. "
Ernest Holmes

"It is an historical fact that privileged groups seldom give up their privileges voluntarily. Individuals may see the moral light and voluntarily give up their unjust posture; but, as Reinhold Niebuhr has reminded us, groups tend to be more immoral than individuals."
Martin Luther King Jr

"We are here to transform who we are as human beings, from a place of wisdom, not desperation."
Dafina Kufica

"The intent of the Creator of life and the living substance is that men must live in harmony within themselves and with one another, and perhaps with all of life."
Howard Thurman

"For as in one body we have many members, and the members do not all have the same function, so we, though many, are one body in Christ, and individually members one of another. Having gifts that differ according to the grace given to us, let us use them: if prophecy, in proportion to our faith; if service, in our serving; the one who teaches, in his teaching; the one who exhorts, in his exhortation; the one who contributes, in generosity; the one who leads, with zeal; the one who does acts of mercy, with cheerfulness."
Romans 12: 4-8

"While I know myself as a creation of God, I am also obligated to realize and remember that everyone else and everything else are also God's creation."
Maya Angelou

ABOUT THE AUTHOR

Tracy Brown
Your Voice and Guide for Inclusion

Tracy Brown is the founder of Stained Glass Spirit. After working for more than 20 years on diversity and inclusion strategy in organizations nationwide, she created Stained Glass Spirit to focus attention on "attracting diversity and creating inclusion" in New Thought spiritual communities. Visit www.StainedGlassSpirit.net for updates.

In addition to her professional experience, Tracy has been a student of New Thought / Ancient Wisdom since 1986. As a licensed spiritual coach, she is uniquely qualified to be a bridge between business best practice, individual responsibility and Spiritual Truth. Her book: "I Turn to Prayer" is a collection of prayers and prayerful poems.

Tracy is an accomplished speaker and author who is known for her ability to engage people in sensitive conversations. While the majority of her work includes all dimensions of diversity and focuses on building a practical strategy for inclusion, she is also well known for her contribution to initiatives focused specifically on race, racism and race relations.

She is the creator of the award-winning process used by Dallas Dinner Table. And, as a result of Tracy's 'What is Mine to Do' TEDx Talk, she began moderating the Mine to Do Facebook Group which challenges people to be proactive to reduce or eliminate race-based hatred and violence.

Tracy has delivered training to more than 450,000 people in the past 15 years. In addition to working in corporations and associations nationwide, she is also a popular instructor for Holmes Institute and Centers for Spiritual Living's School for Spiritual Leadership. Tracy has produced or hosted several internet radio shows, including "Intentionally Inclusive," a podcast specifically focused on what leaders of spiritual communities need to know and do to inspire inclusion.

For more information about Tracy Brown, visit www.TracyBrown.com or www.ReclaimJoy.com

SELECTED BOOKS BY TRACY BROWN

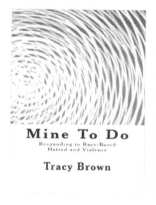

Made in the USA
Monee, IL
15 August 2022

11675188R00077